MORNING STAR

BY

VAL BLACK

BLACK

First Published 2010
By Neville Black
© 2010 Valerie Black

Valerie Black is hereby identified as the author and asserts her moral rights.

Printed by Remous Limited, Milborne Port, Dorset DT9 5EP
www.remous.com

ISBN 978-09567136-0-5

Any proceeds above cost of printing will be donated to Compass Counselling on Merseyside

Foreword

I woke this morning, early as usual, and stepped out of bed without turning on any lights. It was dark. I went to the window to look up at the sky. The previous day I had read through Morning Star at one sitting. My waking thoughts were about the wonder of the morning star piercing the darkness, heralding a new dawn.Lifting the blinds I saw no morning star. Fog pervaded the landscape, but I knew it was there somewhere, perhaps lighting the way for someone else.

Val Black has provided for her readers a new and very personal way of looking at life when it is dark, or when fog removes the familiar landmarks that bring meaning and identity. It is a book of hope. Having come through dark places of physical and mental health herself, she has taken time to share her recollections of what pierced the darkness for her and for others. Having studied, trained and practised as a counsellor for over 30 years, she brings a wealth of experience. She knows how to listen. She pays tribute to those who were there for her in a listening kind of way.

This is a book full of morning stars: of people in and around her Liverpool life. In this celebrity culture where to be famous appears to be what many aspire to, Val Black is at pains to stress that star quality is to be found in what she calls 'us ordinary people'. The sheer goodness, kindness and fun is active in the unsung places, and is under our noses if only we look. For example, we are introduced to Mrs D, who although bedridden for many years, opened her home to all ages. Here, people felt welcomed, comfortable and significant, while she enjoyed their company. Or again, hope can come through a well-timed cup of tea like the one brought to Father Vladimir.

Reading Morning Star is like sitting beside the author with a cup of tea as she tells her stories, naturally and without a shred of self-indulgence or break of confidentiality. Underlying every description is her faith. This has been tested many times, but still remains unshaken. Jesus Christ is clearly her morning star, always there, sometimes hidden in fog, but clearly in the lives of ordinary people very close at hand, including her husband, Nev. All we have to do when darkness pervades is to look up, listen and believe, as she has done. The new dawn will come. Val Black, from her wheelchair, has listened to hundreds of people over the years, herself being a symbol of hope. She has enabled each one to look for his or her morning star at his or her own pace. Now it is time to listen to her.

This book, by the grace of God, will prompt many of us to go on looking for the morning star each day in one another, and in creation, which will bring light and hope when darkness falls. We know that though fog may hide the pin-point of light, it continues to shine somewhere, somehow; a symbol of hope.

Grace Sheppard
Wirral
January 2010

I heard the voice of Jesus say,
"I am this dark world's Light;
Look unto Me, thy morn shall rise,
And all thy day be bright":
I look'd to Jesus, and I found
In Him my Star, my Sun;
And in that Light of Life I'll walk
Till travelling days are done.

Horatius Bonar
1808-1889

Dave, Frank and the Victorian Post Box

It all began with a 'phone call. As usual the Vicarage had been its normal chaotic self..... Neville, my husband, tearing out at an ungodly hour to the London train. Three daughters getting under each other's feet looking for socks, mislaid homework and cornflakes, while I distractedly galloped from one to the other, fooling myself I was being useful and solving the problems.

At last they were gone and I stood gazing at the pile of dirty dishes. Then the 'phone rang. I picked it up and prepared to launch into my usual speech, "Sorry, Nev is unavailable today – can I help you?"

"Uh, that's a shame" said a voice. "It's Granada TV here. We wondered if Mr Black would have been available to make a comment tomorrow morning about the Victorian Post Box".

I struggled to collect my scattered wits and asked, "What's happened to it?"

"Not surprised you don't know," responded the voice "The day before yesterday the Post Office removed it and replaced it with a new one. The old one is to stand outside the main centre in Copperas Hill".

"But why?" I asked baldly

"Well, they wanted one to stand outside the new PO building and there's only three Victorian ones left. One of course is in Woolton........."

I waited for no more. I stormed and raged down the 'phone:
"Typical, absolutely typical. Just because it's unimportant old Everton <u>we</u> don't matter! <u>We</u> won't have the energy to get up petitions and create a fuss."

I spoke of a disappearing landscape and the struggle to preserve something........ Of Frank Green sitting in rain soaked streets painting away before the terraced rows of houses, pubs, churches and cobbles disappeared...... Of Dave Evans, loving his own area so much that after a Cambridge degree he returned to a local junior school and took the children hunting around the area looking for traces of their roots – fanlights over doorways, grave stones, the old round house, Prince Rupert's Well.

"You see", cut in the voice "it will only get vandalised up there on the hill. At Copperas Hill it will be cared for and preserved."

I choked in my wrath!

"You sound very indignant yourself – will you come instead?"

I had said "Yes" and slammed the 'phone down before I gave it another thought. Heck, what would I say? I look terrible on film – whatever possessed me?

The following morning I was standing on the corner of Breck Road. It was freezing. The sort of cold you only find standing on that hill looking out over Liverpool to the Welsh hills when the snow is about to fall. Frank, Dave and I shivered together standing by the hole where the old Post Box had stood and occasionally gazing resentfully at the new monstrosity. After we had stood in those conditions for nearly an hour the camera crew arrived. Amidst apologies about getting lost and comments like, "God it's freezing, let's get on with it", cameras were organised and the interviewer grouped us together.

I know I hardly said a word and was conscious of Dave and Frank keeping their end up and talking away. I found my attention drifting. Looking from the left, way over to Islington and following the broad sweep up to St George's Church, there was hardly a building left standing. Monstrous new high rise blocks already showing signs of wear and tear; piles of rubble were strewn in mounds. The whole atmosphere felt sad and depressing.

Frank and Dave said their goodbyes and raced away. The cameras were packed up and the smart young interviewer was already searching his instructions for the next port of call and "interest of the moment" to which he had been assigned.

I turned my back and hurriedly walked away. Turning the corner my steps started to slow and to my surprise there were tears standing in my eyes. Whatever was all this about? It was only a stupid box. It had even been replaced. So why all this heavy reaction? I began to ponder. What would I have said to that awful camera if I had been really honest and able?

It would have been something like this.

Take a look at this area! A place where hundreds of Liverpudlians had made their home for nearly two centuries and more. It has been a place to struggle for survival. With bad housing, lack of money and resources, men, women and children had been born, married, died, laughed, cried, suffered and celebrated. Clung to families or stayed alone! Belonged to streets, shared their bread, cutlery, loos and fights! Swung on the lamp-posts, played hopscotch on the flags and got drunk in the pubs. Some had even gone to church. Even there there had been some struggles with people moving the fights from a personal basis to a catholic/protestant battlefield on occasions.

The post box symbolised their passing. No-one remembered! The bulldozers obliterated! Frank and Dave were determined they would not be forgotten – their self respect, their courage. Of course we needed new housing, new loos, new shops, new beginnings, but we owed so much to the fighters of the past who had learned how to survive in such circumstances. How many hands had posted their hopes, fears, decisions, communications of all sorts into its open mouth? How many beloved scraggy mongrels had made use of its ample shape?

How many kids played tick around it and how many lovers had leaned against its strength – dreaming dreams?

How many times, I wondered, did ordinary everyday people, doing very simple everyday things shine in the darkness? That deepest dark before the dawn when that tiny starlight quality enlightened the darkest places of people's pain.

I had spent only a short period of my life in Everton, but as I looked back I realised how many people had a hand in my life – people who had died or moved on – people who had contributed to my experience – had taught, encouraged and enabled me. Some were clearly remembered – some forgotten and all making their contribution to my human story. Important and insignificant in one and the same moment!

Maybe this was in my mind when I became aware of the Morning Star for the first time.
By the way you can still see the post box standing outside the Copperas Hill Postal Centre. It is set behind a little walled off area, surrounded by weeds. If you look carefully you'll find it.

The Beginning of the Journey

Working as a counsellor for over thirty years I have been privileged to hear the most amazing stories of courage and survival over adversity. Because of confidentiality most of these stories will never be heard. Oh yes, there are stacks of books written on counselling itself and related subjects. You can now take training courses in teaching establishments all over the place as well as those set up in the counselling centres of the country. Even the NHS and GP practices have their counsellors now. Yet for me, and for many counsellors, the bottom line has to be the people themselves who come for counselling who teach us our job.

During my years as a tutor I must have said dozens of times that people learn about themselves by striving to do amazing things – travelling the world, sailing yachts to Australia, climbing in South America, searching the deserts and jungles for wildlife. Yet I have found the most precious privilege and learning experience has been to sit in my counselling room, working with another human being as he or she takes the risk of the journey within. They struggle to learn how to bear their pain by facing it.

Many, many years ago an incident occurred which opened my eyes. I was working alongside a woman D......, who was allowing herself to revisit a childhood experience which must have been devastating. I can see her face still. She was talking of her utter despair as a little seven year old separated from home. In the early hours of one morning she was curled up on the floor, soaking wet and freezing. Night was at its darkest – always darkest before the dawn. Exhausted after facing memories of truly wicked treatment and a sense of total aloneness she sat quietly looking downward.

Stunned by her story I sat silently with her. I don't know how long. At last I gathered myself.

"How on earth", I asked, "did you survive those terrible hours?"

There was another silence. Eventually she eased her back, sat up a little straighter.

"I was cowering in the corner and something made me look up. There was a skylight and through it I could see just one tiny star."

She stopped and lifted her head as if once more it was visible to her.

"It was so very dark but that one star gave me something to cling to. It was there until dawn began to break".

Again the silence!

I found myself searching. Why, why would that one light in the darkness mean so much that it saved a small child's sanity?

Then I took a risk.

"Who was your morning star" I asked.

A small smile touched her lips.

"Oh, my granddad! I knew he really loved me. Once a week I would see him. He would let me climb on his knee as he sat by the fire. He would put his arm round me and tell me stories and make me laugh".

Another silence!

"He was my salvation".

Since then the morning star person has appeared many, many times. Often the morning star people don't even know what their simple everyday acts have done. What they have given to another person.

The human spirit overwhelms me in its courage and tenacity to cling to life.

There are so many natural disasters and such human wickedness in the world; yet time and time again we can see this desire to make life better, not only for ourselves but for others, ranging
from small African children wrestling with war conditions, HIV, hunger – lacking the very basics of life, to those who have their basic needs met yet strive with the anguish of physical or mental long term illness, to prisoners who suffer brutality with no hope, no power, no control.

The morning star people can make unbelievable difference by very simple acts.

Oh I know we need the amazingly special people – Winston Churchill, William Wilberforce, Edward Jenner, Luther King, Louis Pasteur, Helen Keller, Nelson Mandela.
Where would we be without them?

But my counselling experience has taught me that it is not only the brilliant, the hugely dedicated or the powerful that can change lives. It's the ordinary you and me in our daily lives, caring about ourselves and for the people around us who make such a contribution yet are often unaware of what they have given.

D...... started my journey. I began to look back for the morning star people, those stars of mine and of others.

This is not about my wonderful family and the great friends and colleagues I have been very privileged to have in my life. I couldn't have got by without them. I must add the medical people without whom I would have disappeared years ago.

This collection of reminiscences (mine and other people's) is to try to show some ways in which lives have been changed, or enhanced by the morning star people. Those who bring light in dark places and show us the way forward.

In some instances I use actual names as I have been given permission.

Stories which I keenly want to record but wish to protect my source I have changed names or places.

To D...... who began this journey I would just want her to know how she and so many clients have enriched and enhanced my life by their courage and their sharing.

Thank you.

Ken

Although Bootle was my home, many of my childhood holidays were spent in Prestatyn. My mother was very close to her sisters. Vanda was the one who lived in Prestatyn. She had a son, Roger, two years younger than me. We saw so much of each other that we played and fought as brother and sister might.

Two boisterous youngsters exhausted their mothers' energy and patience. So in the spring, and on summer days, we would be taken for long walks by Uncle Ken. He never seemed to tire of our company and never gave us the impression that we were a nuisance or a bore.

We climbed Fish Mountain scampering in and out of the trees, up and down the shady paths. I would gaze up through the branches watching the sunlight making patterns with the shadows. We would stand very still and hear the birds.

The higher we climbed the more stony the path became and eventually we would arrive at the cave. I'm sure Mum and Auntie Vanda wouldn't have let us take the risk but Uncle Ken would switch on the torch and into the passage we would step. Excited and adventurous we felt, touching the wet stones beside us, paddling through the tiny stream with the occasional drip of water descending on our heads. Weird shaped stones, worn with age, cast their shadows, giving us an eerie feeling as our footsteps echoed.

"Hello!" We called, and laughed at the "Hello-ello-ello" which followed and then merged with the echoing laughter.

Roger and I would vie with each other as to how far we dared to go and usually Roger won. I don't expect we went further than twenty yards, but it felt like miles. Suddenly we would turn and run – bursting out into the warm sunshine with relief and laughter. Uncle Ken would follow behind smiling.

On the way home we didn't run ahead. We pressed close to Uncle Ken's side listening to the stories he would tell of pirates. The sea would have come inland very much higher in early times and the old tunnel would have been used to store ill-gotten gains. Our eyes would sparkle and that night we would go to bed and dream our dreams, deliciously scared yet cosy and safe in our small beds with the family chatting quietly below.

Another favourite walk was to the honeyman's house. It was the opposite way to the hill and took us through the fields, rustling the grass and picking buttercups and clover. To reach the farm we had to cross the old stone bridge. We would hang precariously over the edge to see if there were any fish in the stream. Uncle Ken would often let us go down to the water's edge where the slippery grass and mud would precipitate us into the water – white socks, shoes, best coats and all.

The day I most remember was seeing frogs and tadpoles all at the same time. A tiny frog on another's back and dozens of tiny wiggly things swimming everywhere.

Regretfully we would tear ourselves away and squelch on to the farm. We always waited outside while Ken and the old farmer went in to talk. They would return with eggs in a box sitting in straw. Sometimes there was a jar of honey. I can never remember the farm clearly but we sat on the gate fascinated with the garden. The old lilac tree would be weighed down with blossom with the wild primroses beneath in clusters. But the thing which held me enthralled was the occasional lilac primroses and yellow lilac. How could it be? On the way home Uncle Ken was plied with questions. How, why, what, when? He did his best to explain about the bees and the pollen and how many bees, and how much honey, how the colour changed. I imagine what he didn't know he made up.

Our arrival home to our devoted mums was to be expected.

"Ken where have they been? They're soaking wet! Oh, and to think they went out so beautifully clean and tidy."

Strangely enough I don't remember changing our socks and shoes, or washing the mud off, but I do remember that lilac tree!

As we grew older and into our teens so we became more sophisticated. No longer did we clamour for walks in the country. Now we would be looking to spend time in the local coffee bar or the latest pictures.

Ken became more and more arthritic, his tall thin frame more stooped and stiff. Our times together changed. With Mum and her sister, Vanda, in the kitchen making lunch or tea I would sit on a stool beside his chair listening to him talk of ancient Egypt, Rome – all sorts of things.

I was married and expecting our daughter Mandy when I saw him for the last time. Ken was dying of cancer, lying in the big double room overlooking the back garden.

"He's very sick", Vanda said. She was in the kitchen baking an apple pie. Ken had expressed a desire to taste that lovely "homemade pie".

"Then he shall", said Vanda. Even though we all knew he may not be able to taste it.

I remember very little of that visit but I do remember going up with my Mum and being left for a few minutes to sit on the side of the bed.

"I don't think he knows", Vanda had said.

But as Ken opened his eyes he smiled at me.

"You won't forget our little conversations will you?" he asked.

"I won't forget", I said.

I sat a bit longer, and came away.

That must be over forty years ago. Yet here I am! Unexpectedly remembering with such clarity.

Ken was no plaster saint. He was a man who had faced a hard journey in life. Damaged so badly by his father he would not allow his son to call him Dad – always Ken.

His early life had taken him into the First World War in the Med, on destroyers.

Through an accident which damaged his health he lost his business. Yet he survived to work for many years as a manager of a telephone exchange. His latter years were dogged by acute arthritis. Yet he had received enough in his life (probably from his star people and especially his wife Vanda) to enable him to be a real and caring friend to me and others.

Reading this to my daughter she surprised me with a thought of her own.

"Maybe", she said, "you listening to him and his stories was not just about you gaining by having him give you the message of the morning star that you mattered. Maybe he needed you too!"

You know, I'd never thought of that before.

Annie and her school teacher morning star

Annie has been a friend for several years and although I know something of her present I didn't know much about her past.

Talking star issues one morning she shared a little of her story.

Born into a French family she had an older brother and sister. At the age of ten she was known to suffer from asthma and bronchitis. Annie did not wish to talk of her family and childhood but did want to speak about her morning star person.

Annie had been off school ill and her parents had not told the staff what was wrong. Standing for the register to be called Annie felt very shaky, fearful and ashamed that her parents had not given her a note to explain she had been ill.

Madam Faguer, the English mistress said "Oh! So you have been ill? You know I have a daughter, and I say to her "I wish I had a daughter like Annie". No criticism, simply appreciation. I don't know what it might have done to the daughter but Annie was stunned. She had often felt unease and aloneness – unvalued, low self esteem. Yet this comment opened a new attitude and awareness. An awakening! It did not give Annie anything that she did not have already but it awoke her to see herself in a different way. It helped her to get in touch with those things within her which were waiting to blossom. Having always enjoyed English, she now flourished. She always came first in class. The first book she owned was about two English children and their bikes. It fired her enthusiasm and she loved it. Annie still has it today. Annie began to fall in love with England.

Madame Faguer may not have been aware, but this affirmation of Annie brought about the change. "I felt her soul and she awoke mine" was her comment years later.

Annie grew to love the English language. Her enthusiasm enabled her to take a degree. She came to England and is still in Liverpool today.

Annie made an interesting comment that the brightness of her star disappeared with the dawn.

Madame Faguer died of cancer.

Years later Annie had become deeply involved in the counselling world. In a psychodrama session she found herself remembering her star, and felt her old teacher would be able to come back to defend her if she was needed so strong was the sense of support after all that time.

We can only be ourselves. We have to give ourselves permission to love ourselves enough to fulfil our role in life.

Captain Sharman

During our mid-teens life changed for my friends and myself in many important ways. We struggled towards "O" Levels, acquired boyfriends, and for me a major change of "being converted". It was the atmosphere building up to the Leith Samuel Convention in Bootle and suddenly the years of childhood Sundays spent soberly laying down Biblical knowledge and singing the old choruses was blown wide open. There was a new excitement. Christianity was seeming to take off – vital – alive.

I felt swept along by my friends whose new experience of Jesus was changing their lives and giving them such a challenge. I made my own private commitment although I don't think I fully understood at the time what it was all about. Come to that I'm still only scratching the surface of my spiritual journey even now.

I met a new boyfriend, Nev, inspired and elated by his "finding" Jesus for himself. Together we became involved in Waterworks Street Church Army Mission, street meetings, witness teams and the whole exciting Billy Graham era.

Partly, I guess, it was the pleasure of belonging. It was the teenage peer group, all of a similar age, all throwing themselves into the Christian way of life with evangelical zeal.

I could write of what we did, Church services, our commitment to the Rwanda Mission, the Roy Hession House parties in North Wales.

This is where we were privileged to meet Corrie Ten Boom who affected us all so deeply by her stories of her life in a concentration camp. We sat high on a Welsh hillside, a large group of youngsters, sitting safely around a large bonfire in the twilight, but many of you will have read her books and know of the miracle wrought in that camp – tiny miracles – tiny sparks of light. Her sister though did not survive.

We met William Nagenda, a delightful, dear Christian man who had made the journey from Rwanda to this country to talk of his beloved homeland.

I can remember a day out on the Great Orme in Llandudno. At the top there was a restaurant and just outside was a fruit machine. William gleefully put in his money and began to play. Roy came through the group and placed a hand on his arm smiling and shaking his head. "It's gambling" he said.

"Oh" said William, jumping back – "I didn't know – it's such fun".

He walked away not even challenging what was said.

I found myself chuckling a few months back when Nev found a similar machine at a place where we were having lunch. He had a go and as he laughed I remembered William all those years ago, innocently just having fun.

I'm also considering his attitude to Roy and submissive acceptance of the "decree". Not far enough, but we have come a long way from those days.

The Church Army Captain at the Mission was a Captain Sharman. He was a very nervous anxious man who was completely committed to his God and his work. I don't think he was too keen on me. I think I was a bit flighty and too interested in clothes, and my boyfriend. Nev met up with him just a few years ago in Norfolk, still the same humble, prayerful man he had always been. Nev found out as they chatted that he remembered to pray for each member of that old group daily throughout the years even though out of touch with many of us.

He is the morning star person I have chosen from this era. We heard this story from Nev's Mum – a typical one. The lady who acted as his landlady was most distressed when he came in one evening. A small child of the house was very ill. The doctor had said there was nothing more he could do and said he would come back in the morning. The Captain went to the child who was restless and sweating. He laid hands on the child and prayed. The mother could see an immediate change. The boy became cool, and the restlessness gave way to peaceful sleep.

"Don't tell anyone" Captain Sharman said. "People can make a lot of fuss about these things". It was only a very few people who ever heard about it. Isn't it strange? I don't even find it easy to tell this story. Why? Well, maybe because I am a very logical, down to earth sort of person and I have no explanation; and maybe I feel I won't be believed. We are often scared of what we don't understand. Yet into this book this is going to go as a morning star person who is often unseen and seemingly unremarkable. Yet here I am fifty years later writing about him.

Mrs D

It was during this time we were teaming up with the young people of the next parish. One Sunday evening after church a young lad said

"Hey, are we all off to Mrs D's?"

"Who's Mrs D" I asked.

"You mean you've never been to see her?"

"But you must come".

The group moved off down the street. Not far away we came to Hawthorne Road. A road with blocks of terraced houses interspersed with the bus depot, garages and blocks of small shops.

Behind one of these blocks the group of youngsters turned into the narrow alley. Halfway along someone unlatched a wooden back yard gate and we trooped through the yard, past the outside loo into a tiny gas lit scullery. As I got through the door I stood still. I could see into a kitchen/living room which would have been behind the shop. The gaslight flickered and in the shadows I started to pick out the details. An old black leaded range burned the coke brightly. On top a kettle steamed and hissed. The only visible piece of furniture was an old polished sideboard.

An older man sat in the armchair by the fire with two small girls on his knee.

The rest of the room was filled with chattering youngsters, all talking nineteen to the dozen, sitting on chairs, on the arms, on the window ledge.

Mainly the youngsters were in their mid teens. They were either still at school, training or just starting jobs. Some searching for work, feeling adrift! Lost! From memory we were a mixed bunch – secretarial, electricians, civil servants, banking, carpentry, nursing, shop workers, garage hands. We all managed to find common ground in that kitchen.

This I seemed to absorb with a glance, but then I caught sight of what appeared to be an old sofa in the corner. At first I thought it was just another three or four people squashed on to it. Suddenly I realised it was a bed. The beautifully clean but thin blankets covered a frail form and as I caught sight of her face, she saw me. It was a thin, sallow, sick face, but the eyes were sharp, alive and twinkly.

"Hello. Now I haven't met you before – come and sit by me! You can tell me about yourself! Shove up you lot!"

Shyly I squeezed through and sat beside her. By this time there would have been anything up to thirty youngsters trying vainly to squeeze a place for themselves.

I found myself chatting quite easily to the little woman, but it soon stopped as Charlie brought out his guitar. The room rocked to the singing – hymns, choruses. Someone read a little piece out of the Bible.

A group were making tea and tossing biscuits about. Everybody got fed. At last I stood up.

"I must go. My Dad won't let me be late", I said.

"I should think not", said Mrs D.

"Come and see me again during the week when it's quiet. Then we can have a proper chat."

As my boyfriend and I stepped out of the light and the noise into the quiet, still alleyway I found myself not wanting to talk. Nothing amazing had happened, but somehow my awareness had changed. It was an important evening.

"Isn't she great?" Nev enthused.

He talked on as we walked swiftly along the wet streets. I pondered quietly to myself. My decision was made. Before next Sunday I was going to pay another visit to this lady – on my own – in the quietness.

Two or three days later on a sunny afternoon I again stepped into the dark kitchen. There she was, alone, leaning back on her pillows. There was that little smile.

"Hello", she said, "come and put the kettle on".

No question of why I had come. Just a good old fashioned warm welcome. She was pleased to see me.

In the days and weeks that followed I learned a lot about this most unusual woman.

Mr & Mrs D had lived behind the lock up shop for many years. They had a son Freddie and a daughter Freda. The two younger girls were affectionately known as Spud and Mash. They had been a Christian family for a long time – all except Freddie that is. I had heard from others that Mrs D had heart trouble, and was virtually bedridden apart from the very occasional outing to church in her wheelchair.

On this afternoon visit, after the tea had brewed, I stopped talking about myself and looked across at her as she lay in the shadows.

"Would you tell me something about yourself?" I asked her tentatively.

As she lay back on her pillows her mind seemed to flow back searching her memories. It had all started with her marriage to her "Mr D" many years before. Yet even with their first child, Freddie, there had been difficulty.

She herself was very ill and Freddie was premature. So tiny he needed dolls' clothes. As I thought of present day six foot tall, broad shouldered Fred, I smiled. There was a girl, Freda, and then the twin girls, Spud and Mash.

"Cup of tea, hey?" she requested.

When I had placed the cup beside her, she gave a mischievous grin.

"Open the cupboard", she said, nodding towards the sideboard. I looked, questioning.

"Open the cupboard", she repeated.

There were boxes and boxes of tablets. I raised my eyebrows.

"Years ago", she began, "the doctor told me I was dying. If I was very good, stayed in bed and took my tablets very regularly I might manage another two or three months. What use was that to me?" she asked.

I didn't know how to respond.

"I had four children to raise. I thought long and hard. I was God's child, so I prayed. "God", I said "I want to live long enough to see my children grown and able to look after themselves. I won't take another tablet because I'm going to trust you to see me through".

She looked up at me.

"He hasn't failed me. With help we are getting there." Today with the wonders of modern science, medicine has taken huge strides. There would probably be heart bypass, pace-makers, wonder drugs, which would enable her to leave her little back room. She would have a very different life and ministry. That would be wonderful for her and her family. Yet I feel what could be missed if we aren't careful is that being so taken up with our striving for competence we might lose that warm, natural being with people.

The strength of her prayers was there not only for her family but for all those young people who flocked to her little back room. How many unhappy or worried youngsters poured out their problems to her alone?

I too went to her, my morning star in the darkness, when it was thought my boyfriend had TB because he had a shadow on his lung. It was years later Nev told me he used to go and talk to Mrs D about it. He hadn't told me, but then neither had she.

Nev couldn't believe that I too had sought comfort with her without his knowing.

During the day and often during the night when she couldn't sleep, Mrs D would be quietly praying. The results of her prayers were felt in so many ways.

Freddie, her tall, strong, young son, had been extremely anti-Christian. When the girls went off to church he would spend his Sundays at the stables where the local horse and cart were housed, grooming the horse and mucking out.

One Sunday when Fred was about seventeen he arrived back around five o'clock.

"You're early", said his Mum.

"Yeah – I thought I'd have a wash and go to church".

Up reared Mrs D from her pillows.

"Now Freddie, I won't have you making a mockery", she said.

He took no notice – getting a quick wash. Off he went to church. Fred was a changed lad. Mrs D had tears in her eyes as she said,

"You know I prayed all those years for him and when it happened – I just didn't believe it. My faith after all this time is still so weak. I should be ashamed."

There are so many little legends surrounding her but I will share only one more. One afternoon I'd been sitting chatting and as usual she had the baking bowl on her knee in bed mixing cakes for the oven. Now she was tired. Leaning back she asked me to butter some bread for tea. I took the bowl from her and stood it on the old marble top in the scullery. Thinking I was helping I spread the butter very thinly.

"Whatever are you doing?" she asked as I passed the bed to put the plate on the sideboard.

"Oh, that's plenty" I replied. "My Mum wouldn't put more on than that".

No more was said. Others arrived to share time with her. As I walked home I rummaged in my bag for a handkerchief. My hand closed over something cool and oblong. I drew it out – a half pound pack of butter!

At breakfast time the morning after the night she died, Charlie, the guitarist, came to tell us. Tears in his tired eyes, unshaven, he sat hands wrapped tightly round his mug of tea. He had sat up with Mr D throughout the night.

"You know", he said "as she lay there, knowing it was time, she whispered to us, "I keep thinking of that chorus 'Oh that will be glory for me, glory for me, glory for me. Oh that one day I will look on His face – that will be glory, be glory for me'".

With today's media hype, advertisements, films, TV, shopping, world travel, ambition and drivenness, people can get lost. For many, work and the struggle for survival can be over-whelming. The last thirty to forty years of the twentieth century saw the rise of the counselling world. Everything from basic skills of listening and responding to more complex therapies such as primal integration, transactional analysis, NLP, etc, have been on offer. Now it seems to have become yet another modern day rat race. Accreditation, essential insurance, professionalism has to be in place to cover the requirements of the modern world. Of course this is necessary. Progress in learning, practice and so on has to happen. It is unavoidable. Yet there is a part of me which wonders what we might be losing. Where would Mrs D fit in?

As people move away from the churches, as many have, to start, or not start, their spiritual search elsewhere, I have a real sadness that the baby is being thrown out with the bathwater. Trapped in her little back room it was not a prison, as it could have been. Mrs D had a radiance and joyfulness. There was a capacity to cope with pain and weariness yet have enough of herself left over to give to others. How had she found it? How had she learned to pray, to trust in her unseen God? Mrs D had come to know Him - her Morning Star.

I have always been an advocate of taking any help you are offered! If I am told by my GP to take tablets I unquestioningly take them (may be a bit silly but I fear pain).

I have always felt the real importance of working alongside medical staff with counselling – that one may enhance the other.

On reflection I wonder if Mrs D had such great fear she felt she had to put all her eggs in her faith basket in order to trust it to work. In those years she had found a life of service which she offered alongside her vulnerability, fear, questioning and pain.

The morning star quality seems to come out of our own weakness, pain, stress or failure, as well as those things we deem as our "finer points".

Many years ago we had a missionary family to stay with us. After a week the wife's father died suddenly. I was so keen to help and support the whole family!!! I was going to look after the children, do the shopping and washing while my husband helped with funeral arrangements. Two days later I woke up with flu. Calamity! The wife took over her family and mine as well as nursing me. When I was a little better I wept miserably on her shoulder.

"I was going to look after everyone. I've been useless".

"No", she said, "You gave me a gift of purpose and direction – I thought I was going mad but you being sick and being dependent on me saved my sanity. It helped me put my feet on the ground and get over the shock".

Although to have well known, larger than life figures from whom we learn and grow, over the years it has been people who surround me who have affected me the most. People getting on with their lives, dealing with everyday joys and sorrows. It is easy to feel, with the pressure of today's world, that we are very small and insignificant. What we do, what we are, does not matter. It is no wonder that over the past thirty or forty years the need to be acknowledged and listened to has become so strong that the counselling field has mushroomed to such huge proportions.

This few chapters is my attempt to make contact with one or two of the many people who shaped me, and others, who have generously shared their stories. Their names may not echo round the world but in my life they get Morning Star billing.

Morning Star Quality through Suffering

This heading has become more and more clear as I have written about the star. Very often people who have this quality have faced suffering themselves. They and their family and friends have made, or are making, the journey.

I would like to share some memories of a young 'Young Marrieds' group to which Nev and I belonged in our twenties and thirties. This was when I became aware of how people can become stars through their own suffering. Through our combined experiences as we formed close connections between the couples, we found fun, work, commitment, strength and courage together as can happen in groups . Yet I do want to take one person in particular who exemplifies the morning star quality.

Betty

Betty will want to kill me when she sees what I have written. She is deeply committed to life itself – it is for living. Born into a family of five children I think the others would say she was the mischief. Always, there was some idea in mind – an adventure to chase.

I first met Betty when Neville began a young couples group at St Timothy's, Everton. Full of life, Betty and her elder sister, Pauline, with their husbands, Frank and Joe, joined in with gusto. The hub of this group was a number of women who had grown up in the church and had belonged to a girls' club run by a wonderful woman, Miss Ruby Duckett – another amazing story.

Even today I couldn't imagine myself calling her Ruby, but I guess all the girls would speak of her as one of their Morning Stars. A dinner lady who had never been able to fulfil her potential because in those days although boys had an education, girls were not allowed – it would be a waste of money!!! Miss Duckett used her energy and her skills for others, fulfilling her potential in a different way. She took groups away to camp in Filey, supporting the camp by raising money so that some children whose parent(s) couldn't afford it would get the chance of a holiday.

Helping to make sandwiches for the Sunday School party, I "got my eye in a sling" as the saying goes for spreading salmon paste all over the bread and marg.

"Only put paste in the corners – not the middle. They only lift the corners and they'll never notice! It goes further and we're not made of money", Ruby said.

As time went by we produced quite a few children between the couples. We would go for days out and holidays away, delighting in the fun of being together. I have some great memories of the two sisters, Pauline and Betty, with the youngest sister, Jacqui, as they skipped in the long rope together, played rounders, built sandcastles and paddled with skirts tucked up. Other members of the family joined in.

One very rainy day we hired a double decker bus and went to Tatton Hall. Despite the rain we had a great time. As we trouped back to the muddy field where parking had been set up we found the driver struggling to pull the bus out of the mud. He struggled and struggled.

"Let me have a go", said Charlie, their brother, who was a long distance lorry driver.

"No, no!" panicked the driver. "I'll go and ring the company for help."

Down he clambered and walked away into the rain to find a 'phone. Probably a 'phone wouldn't be a problem in these days, and muddy fields for parking a thing of the past.

Pauline and Betty looked at one another, rain dripping from the hoods of their anoraks. Pauline was the leader. She got madder and madder with the wait.

"Charlie", she said, "get in that bus and get it shifted".

Charlie jumped aboard.

"Push when I say" he said.

People had dragged sacks and pieces of cardboard to give the wheels a grip.

"Ok – Now!" Charlie called.

The whole party, minus the children, pushed. Out came the bus like a cork from a bottle. By the time the driver returned we were on the road with everyone safely on board. There was hustle and bustle as the children were dried off and the remainder of the food distributed. Pauline was still huffing and puffing but calming down.

It was a good group and there would be stories to tell of each couple – of fun, heroism, tragedy, bravery and the commitment that makes couples struggle with the negative parts of their relationship alongside what is positive and good – but I will try to stay with Betty.

Whenever there was a problem Betty was there, sleeves rolled up, ready to look after whoever was sick or take care of their kids. At the age of fourteen she went to a neighbour each morning to help light her fire.

Not in the large income bracket Betty and Frank worked hard at every opportunity which offered. Betty helped Frank with the market stall and did things like selling Avon cosmetics to try to top up the kitty.

Ann and Tony were the first of our couples in the group to suffer illness and death. Both healthy, happy, very attractive young adults starting out in their lives, they were rocked to their foundations when Ann was diagnosed with breast cancer, leaving Tony devastated when she died.

Nell and Sid, and Barbara and Frank were also stalwart members – always there. Nell and Barbara were heavily involved in Ruby's club. In later years Nell ran a weekly lunch club for the elderly and those who lived alone. What light that must have brought to those people in their dark places.

Sid was choirmaster all his adult life. Penny and Wendy, two of our daughters, still tell their stories of those happy years. Singing became a part of their lives.

Barbara was the elder daughter of Mr and Mrs Duckett who, together with Ruby and others, ran St Tim's. Full of energy and enthusiasm Barbara and Frank were so hospitable. Sadly, Frank too died quite young.

I still have recollections of a cheese and homemade wine party at their house. These parties were so popular at the time. Come to think of it that was the night of the grapefruit wine! I have never been a drinking sort of person, although an occasional white wine or Dubonet and lemonade never goes amiss.

My first Babycham gave me a headache, so I was not inspired to go any further. At this particular party of Barbara's, another member of the group, Bob, suggested I tried his grapefruit wine.

"It's only grapefruit. I think it's quite refreshing".

I tasted it.

"Delicious", I confirmed, downing a tumblerful. I was fine, till I stood up!

Next morning I couldn't lift my head from the pillow! When I rang Bob later in the day to tell him exactly what I thought of his refreshing wine, I said "I feel like the bells of Shanon are playing inside my head". A good old Liverpool saying!

He laughed saying it couldn't possibly be the wine. Three weeks later he rang me to say he himself had "tasted" the grapefruit. He now knew exactly what I meant.

Beryl and John were close friends to Barbara and Frank. I can see in my mind's eye John on the beach near Rhos on Sea. Bucket and spade in hand, trousers rolled to the knee, digging up cuins and watching him as he picked them from the shell with a pin and popped them in to his mouth. That evening the dare was "who will try one of John's cuins?

One weekend when we were away as a group at St Asaph we stayed at what was then called The Kinmel Arms Hotel. The children played by the river, and later on, the nearby beaches, while the men played footie. My most abiding memory of that particular weekend was going to Morning Service at St Asaph Cathedral. We walked up the path with mums and dads holding the hands of the young ones or carrying the toddlers. The church felt cool, friendly and welcoming.

I have a sneaky feeling that may be one or two of the little ones became a bit obstreperous as the Service moved on and had to be quietly taken outside, but a sense of peace prevailed.

The list goes on – the sisters Jean and Hilda, who shared baby care and a paid job. Jean's husband, Doug, was a good organiser and on one holiday he arranged the menu's for the whole camp. I don't know how he managed it. Everyone got fed and it worked out just fine – apart from a large amount of cornflakes which we took home at the end of the week. – Perhaps thirty boxes was a bit much.

Bob, of grapefruit fame, and Thelma, another couple, came to be close friends for a life time; as did others in the group. We holidayed together for years, often on a Welsh farm caravan site near Aberdaron. We delighted in farm life. Calves, sheep, lambs and kittens were at close quarters and we even got used to dodging the geese. We remember with much warmth the very welcoming Mr & Mrs Evans, Robin (Mrs Evans' brother) and Gito. We were often welcomed into their warm kitchen for tea and homemade cakes and barabrith.

Don't let people tell you that farmers are all hard hearted. Mr Evans had names for all the sheep as well as cows, including Hilda Ogden – his favourite sheep.

Their children and ours became friends throughout their childhood. Strangely they never seemed to fight – maybe because we had three girls and they had two boys.

We enjoyed many happy times together, on the beaches, tramping the muddy country lanes, and singing as we drove along. Uncle Bob was known for his rendition of "The sun has got his hat on – hip hip hip hooray". And we still delight in The Sound of Music, Joseph, Gilbert O'Sullivan and Ten Green Bottles.

Thelma and Bob were the couple with whom we could relax and laze on the beach together; Thelma and I helping the children to build sandcastles and investigate rock pools. We would walk along the beach, paddling in the water to the shop where the children spent their pocket money and enjoyed ice creams or cups of coffee. Thelma was such a good swimmer and would take the girls into the deeper water while I splashed up to my knees.

The men did their things like Frizbees, Kites, beach rounders and knocking the dickens out of a ball attached to a heavy block by a long rubber string.

The late nights in the caravan when the children were in bed are very happy memories. Out would come the Scrabble board or the cards as we sat in the dusk. Thelma and I have one memory of a very enjoyable evening with a bottle of carrot wine. This was given to us by a curate, Andrew, whose father had made it. Again I make the mistake – oh, only homemade! It was very pleasant and a happy time was had by all.

Yet alongside the holidays and fun Bob and Thelma have always been there for us. As steady and faithful as can be. Their regular church commitment right through their lives has been deeply valued by many. The roles of Church Warden, Lay Reader, Tawney Owl, Sunday School Teacher or Community Worker, this couple are always there – stars by just being themselves.

Who knows how many visits to the elderly, sick or "shut-in's" were accomplished by Thelma and Jean (another stalwart) and later Marjorie, bringing a little light in dark and lonely places. Not out of duty! They just care.

Vicars and their wives can move on, but Thelly and Bob keep going, not only uncomplaining but enjoying the people they are with, even through days of tiredness and too much to do. They offer community and stability.

Fun and teaching went alongside each other in their children's work. We remember the plays written and films and tapes produced, using many hours sorting out background tapes and writing the words.

Bob was also the video man which means we have lot of videos of the group's doings.

Bob never pushes himself but when we are in a fix he's there. An aunt of ours, several years ago, was dying of cancer in Sussex and there was no ambulance to bring her the journey to North Wales so that my Mum and Auntie Vanda could care for her. Bob joined Nev in driving down and making a bed for her in the back of the minibus and helping to get her back home. They are the things that others don't see.

During the last couple of years while our youngest daughter has been ill, Thelma and Bob have regularly sent her cards, keeping in touch, letting her know they care; Thelma with 'phone calls and Bob even going so far as hunting out jokes to send to her.

Morning stars in our daughter's darkness.

Alec and Marjorie were a fun couple, ready for anything. Alec was renowned for his photography which he still enjoys all these years later.

May and Albert saved Nev's bacon several times over his car repairs. Les and Joyce lived in an Everton high rise block with their five children! Nev brought the house down by asking Les "What did you do in the War?" "I wasn't born" was the reply!

Don't I get sidetracked? Back to Betty!

Both Pauline and Betty had little girls who struggled with illness while they themselves coped with lifetime problems.

We have great memories of Joe and Paul on holiday when they would spread a large jigsaw on a convenient table for the week, and their midnight feasts at one or two in the morning.

We especially enjoyed the holidays at a girls' boarding school when we lodged in the garden house and were allowed to pick as many strawberries as we wished from the walled garden.

Our three families – Paul, Joe, Thelma, Bob, Nev and myself – youngest to oldest went swimming in the outdoor pool. We picnicked whilst the children squealed and ran in and out, splashing everyone with great glee.

It was such a shock when Pauline died, so very young, leaving Joe to bring up their four children. Both his family and Pauline's family were there for them. Joe carried on – squaring his shoulders as we knew he would, raising his family without any fuss.

Now Joe has his family fully grown and has his grandchildren to enjoy. What a good feeling when he at long last met just the right girl, a nurse – Chris – whom he married. They are so happy together and share very precious times with their family and friends; and those holidays abroad which bring them back looking as brown as berries. Joe is the faithful one who keeps us in touch with visits and 'phone calls. Chris is a great cook!!

Pat, Pauline and Betty's eldest sister, died; and then their brother. Jacqui, their youngest sister died, leaving Tommy to bring up their little son, Philip. Through it all, although ill herself, Betty kept things going. Physically weak, still she found the strength to care and work hard bringing fun into the lives around her. She was there in the darkness.

Gathering the kids together, and later the grandchildren, she, Frank and

Joe would take them to Formby where they had static caravans. They would spend the summer holidays walking through the woods and down to the beach, playing rounders, having barbeques.

Betty's daughter, Hayley, has had real medical problems with ME and Betty has been there yet again. Maybe too much (?) Us mums worry so, and Betty can't stop being the person she has had to be to get them through and survive. Recently, Hayley's husband David took a sabbatical year in Los Angeles to work at the University. The family went too and have enjoyed the experience so much – even went swimming with dolphins.

Betty chuckled when I rang to say "How are you feeling now they've gone?"

"Do you know" replied Betty, "as we waved them off at the airport a man said to me that I mustn't be upset. They would be fine. Little did he know tears were the last thing! The relief of having them packed and safely off is terrific".

Typical of Betty but I'm not sure I believed her.

I'm not surprised to hear that despite how ill Betty has been, she and Frank went over there for a month to soak up some sun! They both came back full of their wonderful experience and renewed energy, despite Betty's "concrete boots" her feet felt like as she left the 'plane.

A deeply spiritual woman (although she won't be happy to see I have written it) Betty never looks for praise. She makes time to stay in touch with friends sending lovely thoughtful cards and small gifts which cheer people like me along the way.

During these years her body has struggled, and her sight is failing. Betty has always looked the very attractive, smartly dressed woman she has always been. She is delighted with her grandchildren and has been there for both Neil, her son, and Hayley's children in every way she can.

'Life is for living' is Betty's motto. She took me to a calligraphy class; and at the time of writing has got a walking group going. With Betty you never know what's next.

The simple fact is she brings light into a dark place. Oh no! Again I say 'no plaster saint' about someone. Betty can be strong and forceful. The positive side of her gifts has brought light and life and support to many in times of need. The negative part may have been she can occasionally be too pressing or forceful. Yet Bet would never have got through without this part of herself.

So there's our Betty still fighting on and being that light which challenges us to keep going and keep fixed on the light that sees her through, her faith.

I gave this to Betty and asked her to read it and give me her permission to put it in. Her comment was "Gosh, you make me sound like Mary Poppins!!" So I asked her to put down what she might want to add. This is it:

"I have often wondered at why such a lovely honest and true family of three sisters and one brother have come to have such short lives. All the words of only the good die young don't really help. I have often questioned why I had been left behind, and of course there are no answers. One thing I am very sure of is that life is so precious and needs to be lived to the full. The people that we are lucky to have in our lives are the most important things, and need to be cherished.

I have had a share of health problems and came to understand that doctors and medicines can only do their bit, and the rest has to come from us.

I became interested in holistic therapies – mind, body and soul as I would word it – all needs to be looked at. I was lucky enough to be able to do a Reiki course at Liverpool Community College. This was a wonderful opportunity for me to do something new and with a lot of different people of a very mixed age. Having completed the course I was encouraged by my tutor to go on. I enrolled for a Crystal Therapy course. This has been fascinating and crystals are such a natural part of God's wonderful world. I now have diplomas, but it is only just the beginning. I would like to be able to help other people to take up something that they feel drawn to, and open up new opportunities in their lives.

One thing I am more than sure of is that we have to make the most of each moment of our lives even if it doesn't feel like a very good moment, it is a part of our life."

Mike

This is my second friend I'm including under the suffering morning star heading. We have talked for hours over the last thirty years. We began when Mike had gone through a time of great emotional stress and spent some time in hospital. Both Mike and his wife Ann have weathered the stress and strain together, each with their own suffering.

Over these years I have been privileged to spend hours with Mike as we have talked together striving for understanding between us and the sharing of our thoughts. Mike is a reader and keeps me going with quotations to think about as well as being a poet in his own right. I find him quite a quiet humble man with a sense of humour who doesn't seem to recognise what he gives to others.

A church person, he has given lifts to older or less active people, acted as secretary to the church committee, supported his church in many ways. I wonder how many children improved their reading because Mike gave time each week to listen to them read with his quiet gentle attention.

His writing of poems and articles in the local community paper have given many people pause for thought.

Yet I wonder how many people who know him recognise how much of his life has been one of strain. How many people know he was sick every morning before going to work?

Although I know Ann we haven't had the same amount of contact, but what I do know of her is that she would not dream of seeing her life in terms of pressure. She makes the most of things, working hard, keeping in close touch with friends, making the most of holidays.

They both share a great love for their two nieces, Jade and Beth, spending much time with them as they were growing up.

They both stood alongside Ann's sister, Liz, her husband Ronnie, and daughter Jade, when one of the worst things that can happen to a family became a reality. Beth was diagnosed with cancer.

At Beth's funeral the church was packed to the doors and into the street. Such a delightful girl, full of life and enthusiasm for her faith. The service was filled with people who shared their recollections of her lifetime, and the gift they have received by simply knowing her.

Mike and Ann walked the journey alongside – no big sticks. No trumpets – just being there. Isn't that what the morning star is all about? You don't notice it in the light but in the darkness it is there every single day.

Joe

Through my tears I looked around the packed church. All the seats were taken and the space at the back was crowded with people. Yes, I thought to myself, it is entirely fitting that so many people would want to come and pay their last respects, to say goodbye, or just to stand and feel their sadness.

Nev tells me that Joe's funeral was one of the most difficult he had undertaken, such good friends as he and his wife Elsie had been over the years.

Born into a fairly large family Joe spent virtually all his life on the docks. It would be easy to write a whole book simply about Joe.

In his school days he was considered to be brilliant at figures. He was the Headmaster's school monitor from eleven to fourteen. He didn't attend lessons as he had exhausted the capacity the school had to offer him.

Joe's adult life was devoted to Elsie his wife and Stephen his son. All his spare time after his job was given to his beloved church, St George's. For many years a stalwart church warden he kept the place going. Elderly Mr Tempest would pass him and quietly squeeze sweets into his hand saying "These are for you! Don't give them away".

Many dockers Joe worked with used him as their banker saying "Keep this money safe till Christmas – then I won't spend it".

He loved a quiet glass of whiskey with his friend Fred and for many years the two men and their wives would be seen together at social occasions – always immaculately dressed.

Joe could work well in partnership as he did with Warden Graham, and later Charlie. During the time Neville was Vicar at St George's Joe ran the Parish Hour each week and dealt with the organisation of the hatches, matches and despatches. When Neville ran holidays for the parish it was Joe behind the scenes who collected the money and paid the bills. I guess if I asked around there would be numerous people wanting to tell you their tale of Joe.

He suffered greatly from heart trouble and in later years his knee was extremely painful. Joe adored his wife Elsie and would do anything for her. Only two things he found difficult. Firstly holidays! He loved his own home and the thought of sleeping in any other bed did not appeal. The second issue was smoking! Because of his heart it was seriously important to stop. Elsie was great and did her best. In the house smoking was banned but it would seem that he would still have a little puff if no-one was looking.

Our daughter Wendy was being given a lift home by Joe when he pulled out his ciggy.

"Don't tell Auntie Elsie", he grinned.

"Oh yes I will", she replied.

Why is Joe one of my Morning Star people? Well, after our third child I had quite a bad break down with post natal depression. I just felt so bad about myself. Slumped in despair, my husband and the family (Mum, Dad, Auntie Lenna, Neville's family and our friends) coped with our three children, the house, and the parish. One Sunday morning going into church Joe came to meet me. He spoke to me with such respect and courtesy it was like a first pinpoint of light in the darkness.

Joe's honesty would tell you the truth even if unpleasant. One year on Mother's Day I had spoken in church in the Service. Afterwards he told me how good it was. The next year as I spoke again at the same Service I was told quietly but firmly, "That was not helpful for those who don't have children!"

Dear Joe! Who else would respect me enough to tell me? How else would I learn?

I had always been aware of his quiet dignity and concern. Although he had a fun sense of humour, before women there was never any smuttiness, and swearing was definitely "OUT". I had always felt like a lady with Joe. A strange, old fashioned word. But I know many a man or woman who found themselves "lifting their game" because Joe thought they could.

That morning when Joe met me at the church door a glimmer in the blackness made me begin to wonder if I could really pull back up that hill. Perhaps I could.

Joe was no plaster saint. He had flaws like the rest of us. There were issues where he could be stubborn or blinkered and would not change. That was the other side of his coin. Yet his loyalty and devotion to what he believed to be right was unswerving.

Joe died at the age of fifty-four. Elsie was totally bereft. Not long ago we visited Elsie and were introduced to Vun, the wife of their son, Stephen, and their beautiful baby girl, Quinn. As always Joe's photo was standing on the bookcase near Elsie's chair, the single rose in the vase beside it. How he would have loved to see the joy they were bringing to his Elsie; and how he would have wanted to know his daughter-in-law and granddaughter. Yet in the way of this world how do we know that he does not know them? How do we know he is not watching over them right now?

It is still a tribute to his influence that even after all these years he is still remembered for the qualities he had which he shared with others.

Lyn

Knowing I was writing about morning star people a friend told me I should meet Lyn Connolly. She gave me Lyn's 'phone number and I risked ringing her.

After listening to me Lyn offered to come and meet me. I thought at the time it was because I was wheelchair bound but I now know that Lyn is willing and prepared to go anywhere on Merseyside to meet people in their own setting in order to share.

I felt deeply privileged to meet Lyn. I am sure her decision to write a book about her experiences is important. It is also important for me to respect her story. So I will do my best to focus on the morning star aspect and not to attempt to cover all of her special journey.

This story is told from Lyn's point of view although I am aware it belongs to all her family and friends.

Lyn became a Christian at age thirteen and met her future husband a year later. For the last twenty years and more Lyn and Mick have run The Wavertree Church in Liverpool. Her deep Christian faith has proved to be the mainstay of her life. Through the many problems life has thrown at them, including cancer, Lyn has found her Jesus the force for healing and enabling that carried her through.

Lyn speaks of the God who never sleeps and her belief in the triumph of hope over depression. Lyn says that as Christians we are not promised a rose garden without problems. She feels we are not immune to the world's difficulties, yet believes her Jesus will carry her through them.

Lyn's immediate family are Mick, her husband, Joanne her daughter, Sally and Gemma – her granddaughters and her son Paul.

One morning several ago Lyn and Gemma were walking home after their shopping. They were talking about Christian things. Just as they reached the house little Gemma said to her Grandma

"So we can trust God for everything?"

"Yes", Lyn replied, "we can".

They entered the house and there they were met by the Police. They had come to tell the family that Paul, their twenty-eight year old son, had been murdered – punched, stabbed and left to die.

Two weeks' previously in their church they had been praying for Holly and Jessica the two little girls who had been killed by their school caretaker. They had also prayed for their families. Lyn had questioned how would you get through something like that? She was about to find out.

Lyn went upstairs and told her little granddaughter what had happened and then went into the bathroom and shut the door. All Lyn can say is that she felt, through her shock, that God took over. Lyn remembers saying to her God "I still love you".

"You don't know", Lyn told me, "how you'll cope". She just trusted He would bring them through. "Our world had fallen apart yet He never changed". She believed her son to be in God's hands.

Two days after his death Paul was to have picked up the engagement ring he was to give to his fiancée, Isabella. She was a primary school teacher. She still wears his ring.

Paul was known as a gentle and caring man. Well loved and respected by the children with whom he worked. A tribute to his integrity and humanity was demonstrated by the fact that over seven hundred people came to his funeral.

A couple of nights after his death Lyn felt her need was overwhelming. Looking at her Bible she found the verse in Philippians Chapter Four, verse thirteen – My God shall supply all your need.

One night she woke to feel that someone was holding her and remembered the verse – Underneath are the Everlasting Arms. "It was as physical a feeling as that".

These are Lyn's own words as she tells the story:

"It was the end of August and the mornings were still dark. As I put the kettle on in my kitchen I happened to look up, and noticed a bright light. The sky above and below were dark, but the light was in the centre of a line of blue sky. It was so beautiful.

The next morning I came down, it was there again; the third morning I am now looking for it, and there it was again. On the fourth morning I went upstairs to wake Mick. I was so taken with the beauty of the light; I wanted to share the moment with Mick.

Together we looked out of Paul's bedroom window, and Mick said so matter of factly "Oh it's the morning star, maybe God wants to speak to you through it".

I looked up "Morning Star", and in Rev 2 v 25-28 I read and knew what God wanted to say to me.

It speaks in v25 about "holding fast", what you have till I come." It goes on to say about how the overcomer will share in Christ's triumph over all evil and evildoers, and God says "I will give him the Morning Star".

To me, God was encouraging me to hold on to Him in my situation. I would be an overcomer through the help and strength He would give me, and then in v28, I read in my Bible notes:
"The Morning Star" Jesus Himself, heralding the dawn of a new day, is our ultimate reward".
I can't tell you what reading those words did for me that day. Jesus

Himself is our ultimate reward. We will spend eternity in Heaven, the place God is preparing for us, and we will see Jesus face to face.

My heart was encouraged, and the comfort I received that day was incredible. God had put on a show in the heavens just to speak those things to me. He patiently showed me four times until I "got it". Even then, Mick had to spell it out for me. How slow we are at times to take in what God wants to speak to us. I love Him so much for the personal and intimate way He communicates with us.

For Lyn it was an awakening. Very soon after this she became deeply involved with IMPACT – In Merseyside Police and Church Together. Her time has been divided between the different denominations encouraging them to pray for the Police in the area, and acting as an intermediary between them and the police. Between all the members of the group ninety two churches were involved.

Later Lyn became involved with the Sycamore Tree Trust helping with courses for prisoners.

It would seem to the onlooker amazing that this gentle, steady woman could find the strength to turn around the horrors of her pain and loss and bring out of it such positive attitudes and responses to the situation in which she found herself.

Probably for me the most amazing part of it all was that she reached a place where she could forgive. Speaking of her time in the court as the two people responsible went through their trial Lyn felt they showed no sign of remorse. Yet all this time later Lyn can say that she can forgive.

The words I have been left with are a real challenge – forgiveness, restitution, restoration, love and courage. That even with such horrors as the damage or destruction of others there is possibility of change. By forgiving Lyn has released herself from bitterness and resentment sufficiently to get on with her life. For those who did the deed they have to seek change in their own lives if they wish for a new beginning.

Oliver

I have been amazingly fortunate with my family, extended family and long term friends – long term stars. They have kept me going with their love and support – my long term travelling companions.

Many of my morning star people don't even know what they gave me. Some were only there for a brief moment while others travelled alongside for many years having come at a time of great darkness. After all, the star is always there – even when we are out of touch we can wake up early one morning and there it is.

After a very heavy time in my life, after the birth of our daughter, Wendy, I suffered a depressive breakdown. For months I was on medication. All I could feel was blackness. My self image was on the floor.

Neville, my husband, was maintaining not only his first church where he was solely in charge, but also coping with house, nappies, a beautiful new baby and two wonderful little girls who must have been very confused by this changed mother.

Both our families gave us much support. Again, we were so fortunate when I think of how many people have to survive alone – with no family or friends. Yet even through all their loving I still could not break free from the blackness.

With the help of medication I slowly pulled back. There were days when I was blanked out; days when I would enter a shop and the words would not come. I wrote lists to hand to the shopkeeper rather than try to speak. My hands were so stiff from medication I could hardly make my fingers undo the zip on my purse.

When I was more in control I went back to speaking in church at the women's meetings. In those years of the sixties and seventies illnesses which affected the mind created a stigma in society. We were living in a time when, if you could see a broken leg, there was tea and sympathy. If it was an unseen mental or emotional problem there were very few who could cope with it. Anything out of the ordinary was treated with suspicion. You ought to be able to control yourself and deal with it!

Two world wars had produced people too numerous to count who were suffering emotional trauma from all they had experienced. The trickle of perception and understanding began to percolate through to us people in the street who had never heard of Freud or Jung.

In the early 1970s when a counselling unit was being set up in Liverpool, a psychiatrist came to speak to the committee. He stated that after the age of thirty five people were unable to change and it was ludicrous to imagine that anyone could grow emotionally after that stage!! I nearly blew a gasket. I remember saying "I didn't begin to grow emotionally till I was thirty six".

The second half of the twentieth century saw huge change in this field. To such an extent that now every crisis reported by the news can have an addendum stating that counsellors would be available for those in distress.

Oliver entered my picture around 1973/4. The counselling world had begun to wake up. Frank Lake had created a group called the Clinical Theology Association which was training people in human resources, pastoral care and counselling.

No longer was the Christian Church closing its mind to possible intervention into this field of endeavour. We found ourselves not only looking back at thinkers and carers through the ages (people as disparate as Julian of Norwich and Paul Tournier) but at the possibilities being presented right now.

Frank's work drew us forward encouraging us to look at everything from pre-birth and post birth to how the human psyche worked. How, in Christian terms, Jesus met each human being where he or she was, rather than where He might want them to be.

Dereck Hall a Liverpool Clergyman, started courses in the area. He persuaded a trained therapist with the Association to travel weekly to Liverpool for the purpose of counselling and training. Just at that time I spoke at meetings and found myself talking of my experience of depression, strongly stating it was no different to breaking a leg or having diabetes. It was not something of which to be ashamed. Virtually each time people would come to me afterwards asking for help.

"I feel just like that. Can you help?"

"My auntie is in this stage – can you help?"

I couldn't even help myself.

At this point I picked up a diocesan leaflet from my husband's desk. There was an advertisement for First Year Clinical Theology training beginning the next week. I thought I might be too late to join but I rang. Was there any space left?

"Yes", said Dereck. "Come next Tuesday and bring £25 course fee with you".

Sadly I put the phone down. On a curate's pay, with three children, there was no way we could afford it. My prayer that night was "If I'm meant to go, Lord please provide the money".

I don't know where you stand on issues like this with so many needs in the world, but next morning there was a letter addressed to me in the post containing £25. It had been posted before I had even prayed.

A morning star person I had never met and never did meet had provided the means.

So the next Tuesday I attended the first session.

Oliver was the tutor. He swung into the car park of the convent opposite Alder Hey Hospital in his old MG sports, hat on the back of his head. His sports jacket bore marks of hard wear with its leather elbow patches.

That evening out of my blackness I could register his confidence. He neither feared nor ran away from emotions. His faith in his God and his belief in the process of counselling gave him strength.

It was as I sat listening to Oliver describing depression that a tiny bright light switched on in my darkness. He was explaining what was going on in my head and my heart! The whole evening is as clear to me today, thirty odd years later, as it was on that night. The warmth and unconditional acceptance of the group was overwhelming. I could cry, shake, talk, not talk – just "be". The Morning Star lit the darkness.

It was not only myself who started a journey that evening. I still have close friendships forged at the time. The one thing that stood out from that evening was something Oliver said.

"If, in these two years, I can enable you to learn how to listen you will be worthwhile counsellors".

I am still learning how to do so.

Alongside training I had counselling for myself with Oliver for eighteen months. I faced my pain, fear, anger, hurt and despair. I started to grow up.

These days counselling is considered to be an important part of training. If I don't know myself how can I strive to separate my journey from that of the client?

How I hate words like "client". Wouldn't it be nice to be able to call someone a fellow traveller or some other mushy term? Ah well! I guess "client" holds us to more disciplined boundaries.

To pack so many years into a few sentences is virtually impossible. I am told the art of being a good writer is to know what to leave out as much as what to put in. Even more important – when to stop.

Oliver told me recently that sometimes he felt he was watching himself when he listened to me counsel. I modelled myself so closely on all he taught me. It was only when we stopped working together when his time of training in Liverpool came to an end that I found myself able to let go and start to trust my own instincts. Yes, my ground was solid. But we are all different, bringing to the task our own special gifts <u>and</u> mistakes. After all we learn more by our mistakes than when we think we are on a winner.

Another thing Oliver taught me was that no one is perfect. We each struggle with our own personalities and agendas. Yet, alongside that, we have something to offer. A person coming for counselling wants to meet a human being – not a robot.

When Neville was at College we both took part in a London East End Student Mission run by Canon Ted Roberts. On the first morning we were introduced to the Bishop of Stepney, Bishop Lunt. Keen and enthusiastic, we all thought we were going to change the world. The old Bishop smiled gently at us.

"You know the people of the East End are used to being loved by their clergy" he said. "I would just offer you this prayer in the hope that you will use it"

"Bring to me today those who need what I have to give, and help me give it"

Here I am today still using it. What a star moment that was! It was only much later when I learnt I could only be me and with limited resources. It is OK to say "No" if I haven't the strength.

In the early days I was swept along – my life being turned upside down. I had the conviction that all people could be healed. Nev used to call it my "Messianic period"! I have learned so much more since then. There is no magic wand! It is a struggle to try to have the humility (and the honesty) to know you can only offer what you have, and trust the other person to be who they can be – whatever that may mean.

Listening quite recently to people who remembered the early days builds quite a picture.

"Oliver? Oh yes! No namby pamby counselling here! He took no prisoners!" Hillary said with a smile. "He told it straight and never evaded an issue".

It was true.

As one woman told her story Oliver broke in to say "Are you sure there isn't another woman?" He was firmly assured there was not. Yet in time the truth came out and I believe she was more prepared to handle it because of the earlier challenge.

Oliver, I believe, had acquired his defences and his strength through his private life journey, his attempts to work on his own material and his belief that God and the process worked. He gave us a list of hurt, longing, anger, fear and despair to use when helping people to trace their emotions.

As with everyone else his own stuff could get in the way. Sometimes his anger or seeming coldness could push someone away. Yet his perceptive skills and disciplined way of working were exceptional. I feel quite cheeky trying to write these comments – almost patronising. This is not so. I began my description by quoting that statement "He took no prisoners". It's true. Oliver expected a good working relationship. He expected his clients to face themselves and trusted they could do so. A client, because of that strength, could raise their own strength and breathe into places of terror, aloneness, hurt, loss, anger or despair in the very depth of their being. He could be firm but in their pain I have seen him be so very gentle and patient.

Often in these groups people find enough courage to trust their counsellor or group leader and revisit painful areas of their lives. It is sometimes necessary in order to release blocked emotions, to try to process confusion, relieve pressure and integrate the experiences in such a way that we can try to learn how to live with them; yet continue to live in the present. I have seen Oliver sitting quietly on the floor beside a distraught man or woman being the strand they clung to whilst they struggled through, being the voice, or hand on the shoulder which anchored them to the present, till they could again take hold of their own strength.

There is so much of the story of primal integration therapy to which Oliver was committed. So much which could be told of his group work, student training and one-to-one counselling. People who were reached at that time are still working in and around Merseyside today.

Oliver had a fun side and could relax. He used to stay for a night once a week after the training group. I would go off to bed leaving Neville and Oliver to settle down together with the TV and a bottle of Scotch to watch Question Time. They would often have times when they would tease and torment each other, interspersed with heavier conversations about world affairs, spirituality, counselling and society.

I have written a lot under this heading, but that Morning Star moment which came in the blackest time of my life was a life changing experience for not only myself but my husband and family who had been coping, somewhat desperately, working to keep everything together as well as struggling with me and my despair.

Morning Stars in Fun

Father Colin

Of necessity the world of counselling is often serious. Yet some of the best moments in teaching can be reached with humour and fun.

I have a very special memory from the early days when a group was away at a convent having a training weekend. One morning we decided to do a well known trust exercise. The group split into twos. One partner was blindfolded and the other was expected to introduce their partner to their environment – trust building!

Most took the task soberly. "Take care!" "There is one small step here". "This is a tree". One couple was different. A Church of England priest, Father Colin (Oxy to his friends) and a Catholic nun, whose name I'm ashamed to say I can't remember (although in my mind's eye I can see her face) Both worked in the heart of Liverpool's most distressed areas at the time of the 1981 riots and had arrived looking weary and both had that strained, exhausted look with the little tell tale lines above the nose.

Believing the exercise was intended to introduce a variety of challenges to trust, the nun crossed her wrists and took hold of the clergyman's hands and started swinging him round and round – a childhood twizzy! They were both laughing and breathless, both delighting in going faster and faster. As they slowed to a stop she hauled him after her down the long garden. She gave instructions when to bend his head as they raced in and out of the overgrown bushes.

At the bottom of the garden was the home of a local priest. The nun bade our priest be silent and had him bend so low they couldn't be seen above the window sills. They were unable to stop their giggling. Suddenly a window shot up and an angry face peered out. Up shot the nun!

"Oh please don't be angry" she smiled, "We're only playing".

They both turned and ran the full length of the garden, laughter burst from both of them in great gasps.

The lines had disappeared – stars for each other.

These weekends were quite unpredictable, but could be hugely growth enabling. My hard, tense shoulders and goody two shoes image was slipping. I had an hour with a counsellor at an Oxford College – a very awe inspiring place. Even whilst working with extremely distressed people and feeling the seriousness of the task I also needed to find my own free child.

I felt joyous and relieved as I came out into the sunlight and gazed at the immaculate stretch of clipped green lawn with its notice "please keep off the grass". I kicked off my shoes and ran all over it. Only those who knew me at the time would realise how huge a step this was for me. I never broke rules – even today my anxiety can make me extremely obedient. At least I had the decency to kick off my shoes!

I never saw the counsellor again but that one hour was sheer star quality opening me up to have permission to let myself play.

Bren

The counselling world can put you in touch with some amazing people, both counsellors and clients. In the privileged position of counsellor you learn about some of the best and worst traits in human nature.

It is often a most humbling process to sit alongside men and women who find the courage and tenacity to face themselves and their situation with real honesty. People who struggle to make progress – to grow – despite physical, mental, emotional or spiritual damage. I could fill a book three times over with the stories of such people who, by their journeys, have challenged me to find courage, to risk, to keep going. But the confidentiality accorded to our clients means we cannot share many of those wonderful journeys with others.

What of the counsellors themselves? Us ordinary human beings who have the temerity to risk placing ourselves in the counsellor's chair! We have our own journeys to manage, our own imperfections to cope with as we try to sit alongside others honestly and equally, offering what we have been trained to do and trying to keep our own personal business clear from the client. As with every sphere of life some do a better job than others as we try to deal with the mixed motives that drove us into counselling.

I have thought long and hard, and have decided to include one counsellor story. I am writing about this counsellor because of her honest hard working human endeavour which keeps her moving forward despite the odds.

I met Bren over thirty years ago on my first counselling training course. Very neat, very tidy, very tense. Married with a young daughter Bren had decided to do some pastoral training for her role as a C. of E. Vicar's wife. We were both struggling towards a better understanding of ourselves, me taken up with acute anxiety depression and Bren very much the creamy skinned ice maiden shielding that delicate, fragile, sensitive centre. We became friends.

Brenda showed a real ongoing determination to work to become the person she could be and to train herself for a counselling role. Training courses, one-to-one counselling, growth groups, and practice steadily took her forward.

During those years she had to deal with a very stressful situation with her husband's job as a clergyman. They were both under pressure with Bren feeling like a fish out of water and her husband Ken off work through an operation which should have been simple yet turned out to be a much longer job than expected.

In the end Ken decided to leave the Ministry. They had to move house as their home was attached to the job. Then Ken left. Never having had paid work since leaving Bible College she had to find employment which was compatible with caring for her little daughter Katherine. She managed to buy her house and maintain a small car.

Through the years Bren has shown great commitment to the counselling unit for which she works. She often did the mundane boring work of committees, washing towels, putting toilet paper in the loos. Many of us just did the basics because all we wanted to do was counsel but there were those who, like Bren, were seriously sacrificial in time and money to create an excellent training and counselling service. Nearly thirty years on Bren has now very happily re-married and became director of the service (recently retired).

Once in a position like this it is amazing how much is expected of you. People are all too keen to say "You don't do this – you are no good at that – why don't you ...." I admit that I too have done my share of pressurising in my time. Bren has withstood it all. Not always right and not necessarily having all the skills, yet keeping the show on the road, looking for people to offer their skills to complement hers, she has kept going through economic pressure. Holding together a staff who strained to keep up with the daily pressure of dealing with queries, complaints, paperwork and figures; looking for ways to reach out to those who would not otherwise have access to counselling.

My guess would be that because of the pressures of the role (and the counselling itself which is often dealing with very heavy material) there are sides to Bren which are not seen in her working role. She and I came through training together. When away at training weekends and conferences, as an antidote or reaction to some of the very desperate emotions that can be dealt with the groups would have a change in the evening when the day was done. Our serious adulthood could give way to a free child. Laughing at nothing, telling jokes, lounging and listening to music, having a quiet drink. Emotions and experiences in themselves were strong and trainers would refuse to work with anyone "under the influence". We shared the joys and pain.

The unexpected often occurred. One weekend the two male leaders were being their usual, disciplined, boundaried selves. At the exact moment of the stated end of a session they would get up and leave until the next session began. It was supposed to teach boundaries and give clients confidence that they could contain feelings and learn to manage themselves.

We slept in dormitories and one particular morning I had just come back from the bathroom when someone flung herself at me. I toppled back onto my bed with a sobbing girl in my arms. We sat and I did my best to steady her and defuse some of the overload of emotion which had gathered during the night. On the way downstairs to breakfast I fumed about "bloody men" and their unrealistic disciplines leaving others to pick up the pieces. Bren was smiling.

"Don't you smile" I responded, "It's the first time in my life I've ever counselled with my knickers round my ankles!"

We arrived in the dining room laughing fit to burst. The laughter took me out of the heavy, responsible place and let me relax.

Bren has a full life of her own with husband, family, friends. A lifetime member of her church, a love of music and the choir to which she belongs – these things may not be to the forefront in the counselling unit. Nor do I imagine many know of such things like the very regular supporting visits she made over several years to a very elderly counsellor who had been a founder member of the unit.

I have chosen Bren to represent the morning star quality of a person who, like the star, is never necessarily noticed in the daylight. Yet when the shadows and darkness are around, just goes on shining quietly in its strength. Bren may not be perfect but she is always there.

When Brenda read what I had written she wanted to add one of her own morning star stories.

> "In the late spring and early summer of 1991 I was in a pit of depression – the most horrendous experience of my life. I had withdrawn from most of my usual activities, including singing in the church choir.
>
> One Saturday a lovely bouquet of peach coloured flowers was delivered to my door by a florist. When I looked at the gift card, I found that it had been sent by the choir. I hadn't been to church for weeks but the next morning I found my way there. I'm not sure how I managed that, but I did! It seemed to me that I could not fail to respond to the love which came with the flowers, and I was drawn back into the church by that love. That was the turning point in my depression and from then on I very slowly came up out of it."

Momentary Morning Stars for Young and Old

Father Vladimir

This man's story comes very near the top of my morning star tales, one that I remember with great clarity for the effect it had upon me. I cannot for a host of reasons share the bulk of it, not least of these being confidentiality. One small incident, one snippet, jut fits the morning star stories so poignantly that I am asking permission to include it.

Having been arrested by police for Christian sympathies and taken to a police station in Moscow, Vladimir was terrified and alone. Sitting in the cell, despairing, he was interrupted in his thoughts by the door being unlocked. One of the men came in carrying a mug.

"I've brought you some tea" he said.

This thoughtfulness helped to bring a tiny light of hope into this dark place and carried him through those first awful hours.

Vladimir had to spend time in the KGB Lefortovo Prison but today is a free man, living his life in a different country, with his wife – a different life for them both.

His whole story I found so humbling and I can't write it, but it did amaze me how such a simple act as making a mug of tea could bring relief and hope into a most terrifying experience.

Desmond and Trevor

I hear that this story has been told many times by the young boy, and repeated by many others impressed by it.

A young boy was walking along the road with his mother. It was the time of apartheid in South Africa. If a black person met a white person the black person had to step off the pavement into the road to allow the white person to pass.

Coming towards the young black boy and his mother was a tall white man in a dark suit and hat. Before the mother could take hold of her child's hand to move off the pavement the man himself stepped off the pavement. As they drew near the man tipped his hat in a gesture of respect.

"Why did the white man do that?" asked the boy.

"That man is an Anglican priest. He is a man of God and that is why" replied his mother.

The young boy was Desmond Tutu, now an Archbishop. The man was Trevor Huddleston; both great anti-apartheid campaigners.

Today, the Archbishop says that the ordinary people are the real heroes.

The Man on the Bus

This second story is about an "oldie" – my Mum and her man on the bus.

This is to show how a chance meeting with a total stranger can bring light and new life.

After the death of my Dad, Mum was devastated. Their life together had been long, weathering the loss of two children, war, loss of parents, sisters and brothers. So to lose her partner at a time when they were hoping for a happy, peaceful retirement was infinitely sad. They had just sold the old family home, a semi-detached in Bootle, in order to go to their retirement bungalow in Rhyl near her sister. She lost her old neighbours and friends at a time when she needed them most. Her sister Vanda and my family (my husband and three daughters) were supportive in every way we could yet for Mum the blackness kept crowding in.

About eighteen months later going into Rhyl on the bus for the aged she met a man. They got talking and she told him her sad tale.

"I feel I've lost my life", she said.

"Well, you know," said the old gentleman, "if you will forgive me? I know it is hard but life will not come to you! You have to go out and get it".

Mum was shocked. It felt, she said later, as if a light had gone on.

"Good day to you and good luck" he said as he left the bus.

Mum sat and thought hard. This was like waking up to a fresh new day. She got down to the pavement and instead of going into Rhyl centre she turned the opposite way up Vale Road to the WRVS Club. Squaring her shoulders she walked in – very nervous but determined. A member came forward saying hello and could she help. Mum told the tale of her loneliness, the man on the bus and asked if she could join.

"Well we are full but goodness! You have been so brave to come by yourself." After some discussion with other members of the committee the woman came back.

"We are going to make an exception" she said.

For the rest of Mum's life the club became a central feature bringing her interest, outings and more especially her own new friends.

Mum never saw the man again and yet remembered him. "He brought light into my darkness", she would say.

Aloneness is a very hard thing to carry. We all in our hearts long for unconditional acceptance and people who care about us. All my life I have been spoilt. I have family and friends. I cannot begin to imagine having no support. Yet there have been times of feeling alone even with others.

So many people these days are forced to struggle on alone. How can they find the morning star people to care? I don't have the answers – I wish I did. All I know is from my Mum. She listened, took her courage, took a risk and it worked. For some it might not, but maybe if we commit to living, and reach out there may be something a little better than there is at the moment.

Morning Star

I have a star that shines for me.
When I'm alone it smiles at me.
It sails on the clouds
And giggles with the moon
It takes me with it as it dreams.

It shimmers with hope
as it whispers to me.
It twinkles with love
As it shines above.

Wendy Black

Endings and New Beginnings

As I come to the end of this chapter in my life I have re-read all that I have written and several things stand out as "missing".

Firstly our time at World Friendship House, an overseas students hostel, with Canon Sidney and his wife Cicely Goddard. Here both Nev and I had a chance to take a good look at the Inner City problems which came to be of crucial importance to both of us.

Neither have I spoken of our years when Nev was in college and I worked in a girls' boarding school as a matron.

Nor have I touched on all our clergy friends and the St Luke in the City years.

All this I feel belongs to Nev's special work and commitment to the multi deprived areas of our cities. Maybe that is another story.

Secondly I have become more and more aware of the thread running through the whole story – my husband and life partner, Nev. Boy and girlfriend from the age of sixteen we have been fortunate to hang on to each other through all the years. In our early days together my Mum said, "It'll never work! They fight like mad".

She was right about the fighting. We have both been strong people prepared to fight for our corner yet we have fifty wedding anniversaries to our credit!!

Without Neville I would have had no contact with St Tim's, Everton; I would never have met Dave Evans and Frank Green; never have met Mrs D. The Young Married's Club would never have been formed. We would not have gone to St George's and we would not have met Joe and Elsie.

It was Nev who supported so strongly my counselling. The life-changing Oliver would have been missed. Bren and I would never have struck up our long friendship.

His ideas, enthusiasm, his ability to make things happen are well known. Nev has an abrasive quality which you cope with or hate. The fact he still has so many friends would say a lot do see through to the man he is.

Nev always says it as he sees it. Over the years he has mellowed a little, and he has certainly wrestled with his own growth and development, and in later years bouts of illness.

Nev's love of people and commitment to his church, his concern for the Inner City poor, Liverpool and Liverpool Football Club have never faltered.

Those who have seen Neville aggressive and challenging, in one-to-one, or meetings, may not have seen the other side to him; for example sitting for a very long time with a mother nursing her dead baby – just being there – no words; or supporting a colleague, sometimes for years, when they were in trouble or alone in their work.

Thirdly I want to speak of the most important people we share – our three girls their partners and their families. They are such good kids and we are so proud of all three. Each with their own journey of fun, joy, sadness illness and pain they fight on with courage doing their very best to make life good for themselves and those around them. They give us so much.

So here I am at the end of this present part of my journey.

Pondering with a friend we asked ourselves what does the Morning Star give us and what does it call us to do or be? The words we came up with were as follows. We can receive hope, light in the darkness, warmth, comfort, purpose and direction. It can give us an awakening, a challenge, recognition of our uniqueness, a life change. Any or all are possible.

I hope this piece of writing will encourage some memories of the Morning Star for the reader.

Our lives are made up of body, mind, emotion and spirit. This has drawn many to work in as holistic a way as possible, seeking to integrate ourselves into a whole being.

I have attempted to incorporate these four areas and know, for myself, the spiritual aspect is what holds me together.

In my counselling these days I am asked if I can work with a person of differing faith, a person who is Muslim, or Buddhist, or those with no faith. It is perfectly possible with respect on both sides and can be deeply enriching.

My Morning Star is the Jesus who has given me all the things I have written about and strengthens me when I attempt to stay with those who find their light from elsewhere. People matter and it is for us in our own ordinary way to try to give the little we may have to offer.

I have to finish by mentioning some names not already included:

Bakers' Dozen	for long term friendship, sharing, challenge and commitment
Joy and Bob Dickinson	for longstanding fun, shared work, stimulating conversation and challenge!!!
Eileen Golbourne	for all her hard work, keeping me and many others supplied with books
Grand Children Jacob, Jorge, Brogan and Ellie	Sheer delight
Bishop Peter and Jill Hall	always there – encouragers in the heat of the day
Jim Hart	who made me write a training course for non wordy, non book people
Michelle Hinchcliffe	for helping me believe I could write
Jacob Lewtas	for patient corrections on the computers
Marie Mckee	for typing and translating my notes!
Medical staff and carers	without whom I would not be here
Rev Michael Morris	who asks for nothing, yet gives his gifts – computers, teaching, CDs, photography, grandchildren support. A man who is unashamed of his love for Disneyworld!
Rev Eddie O'Neal	who has given long term support, especially during illness

Ellis Roberts	My long term friend and supervisor – stalwart, wise, steadying, challenging
Margaret Rogers	for caring, sharing and support
Sister Janet Rourke	When four men refused an inner city parish she came. She reflects all that is good about the Church Army: care of the individual, hard work and honesty. She worked with Ronnie, her husband, at Spitalfields Crypt. Even when he died, she picked herself up and on she went. Well able to take Ordination, she did not feel the need but continued with all the tasks involved in running a church. A good friend.
Angela Ryan	for friendship in our field of work and continued unfailing work with the Bridge Foundation (once CTA)
Sandra, Joe, Keith and Paul Steen	who show us what living the Christian life is all about
The Thomas Family	who gave what they had and made a huge difference to the Black Family
Patricia Williams	a worker for integrity and justice. Family friend and supporter - unstinting with her skills
Canon Dick Williams	for support and proof reading
Canon Michael Wolfe & Mrs Brenda Wolfe	or long term care of our whole family and Mandy and Phil's wedding! All those hospital visits!

Tracy, Fiona, Evelyn Davis   for unfailing friendship and support
and Joan Clarke

Isn't it amazing how many people we may find we need to thank?

Take heed to the light that shines
in the dark place,
until the day dawns and the
day star arises in your heart.
2 Peter ch. 1 v. 19